Hinton Ampner

HAMPSHIRE

A souvenir guide

✿ THE NATIONAL TRUST

20TH-CENTURY GEORGIAN

Hinton Ampner is very largely the creation of one man – Ralph Dutton. It reflects a 20th-century connoisseur's vision of a historic country house estate, expressed through his passion for comfortable Georgian living.

The quiet connoisseur

Ralph Dutton (1898–1985) had unhappy childhood memories of his grandfather's gloomy Victorian house. Like many wealthy aesthetes of his generation, he looked back nostalgically to the 18th century – 'the Age of Splendour', as he called it. He remodelled

Hinton Ampner, which became a sympathetic setting for the fine 18th-century paintings, furniture and other works of art that he acquired. Although he lived a quiet bachelor life, collecting, writing and travelling, he was always a generous host and an understanding landlord to those who lived and worked on the estate.

A unified whole

Defying the chalky, alkaline soil and exposed setting, Ralph Dutton brought together landscape, garden, house and collection to form a sensitive and unified whole that was very much in the 18th-century tradition. But in laying out the garden in the 20th century, he had a much greater variety of plants at his disposal than his 18th-century predecessors, relying particularly on the expertise of the famous Hampshire nursery, Hillier's. He preferred their colouring to be in a low key, avoiding harsh contrasts.

Ralph Dutton began by planting trees in the parkland in the early 1930s, skilfully accentuating the modest undulations of the landscape, and creating splendid views before there was a true focus for them. He followed this by laying out the Sunken Garden in 1935 and so channelling the main view from the house into the South Park, before ultimately rebuilding his grandfather's Victorian pile to

Above Marble urn in the first-floor corridor

Right Ralph Dutton managed to rescue some of his possessions from a disastrous fire in 1960

Creating tranquillity

'I have learnt during the past years what above all I want from a garden: this is tranquillity.'

Ralph Dutton, *A Hampshire Manor* (1968)

Right The garden was designed to embrace spectacular views of the wider landscape

exploit these features. The Sunken Garden effectively conceals the bounds and at the same time bisects the east–west axis, which spans the breadth of the site and is centred on two trees which predate the garden. On either side of this Long Walk, borders were planted over the years. During the Second World War the Lime Avenue, dating back to about 1720, was incorporated into the scheme of the garden, and the planting of substantial shrub-rose borders was inspired by a visit to Sissinghurst in 1950. Another feature which he adapted was the Dell, a chalk-pit which, although first brought into the overall design immediately after the Second World War, proved very difficult to plant and maintain, and probably reached its best only after restoration in 1991.

Ralph Dutton created a series of linked areas with subtly different atmospheres similar to the garden 'rooms' of Hidcote and Sissinghurst. Despite the superb formal structure defined by the hedges and topiary, he never sought to confine the visitor in compartments, but preferred to lead his guests gently from mood to mood, manipulating them imperceptibly by providing deliberate glimpses beyond and by opening areas out, in order to create a garden which encourages contemplation through movement and active experience.

Below A *pietra dura* panel from a table in the Entrance Hall

HINTON AMPNER TRANSFORMED

Surprisingly enough, the house you see today is the newest in the care of the National Trust, built in the 1960s. But this is only the latest in a complex series of transformations.

From Tudor to Georgian

The first of Ralph Dutton's ancestors to live at Hinton Ampner was Sir Thomas Stewkeley, who took a lease on the estate in 1597. He occupied an E-shaped house which had been built earlier in that century about 50 metres north of the present building on a ridge looking south over the gentle Hampshire countryside. The haunted Tudor house survived until 1793, when it was demolished to make way for a plain yellow brick Georgian box, which forms the core of the present Hinton Ampner.

From Neo-Tudor to Neo-Georgian

In 1867 Ralph Dutton's grandfather remodelled and enlarged the Georgian house in the neo-Tudor style and created a garden of formal parterres below it. As a lover of all things 18th-century, it was not surprising that Dutton should have dismissed his grandfather's rambling, creeper-wreathed Victorian mansion as a 'monstrosity of exceptional hideousness'. As soon as he inherited the estate in 1935, he decided to demolish most of it, despite the growing threat of war: 'I was still young enough to take no notice of sensible advice.' With the help of the architects Lord Gerald Wellesley and Trenwith Wells and of old engravings, he sought to reveal the Georgian core of the house and give the whole an 18th-century appearance.

Ralph Dutton was more complimentary about his grandfather's garden ('quite an attractive example of mid-Victorian design'), but remodelled it to create something more in keeping with his neo-Georgian house. Work was interrupted by the war and not completed until 1960.

Rising from the ashes

On Sunday, 3 April 1960, Ralph Dutton was out walking in the park, when he noticed a thin column of smoke rising from the trees.

Below The Victorian house

Pleasant and practical

'Had I been young perhaps a house in contemporary idiom would have shown more enterprise, but I was not young, and a Georgian fabric was essential as a setting for the furniture and objects which I had every intention of collecting to replace all I had lost. Unquestionably, too, rather spacious eighteenth-century style rooms are both pleasant and practical to live in.'

Ralph Dutton

Right The south front of the house today

Vogue Regency

This was one of the many stylistic labels invented by Osbert Lancaster to accompany his visual history of English taste. It perfectly defines the style of interior favoured by Dutton and his circle: late Georgian decor revived, but reinterpreted in the light of 1930s Modernism – smart, sunny, comfortable and spare.

He returned to find the house in flames. His fine 18th-century fireplaces and his collections of pictures, furniture and books were almost entirely destroyed, but, undaunted, he at once began to rebuild the house in neo-Georgian style and create a new collection with which to furnish it.

A generous gift

In 1982 Ralph Dutton succeeded his cousin as the 8th Lord Sherborne, and on his death three years later he bequeathed the estate to the National Trust. The hamlet of Hinton Ampner, the house and the fine gardens and collections were all included in this generous gift.

THE APPROACH

❶ THE PARK

Ralph Dutton believed the ancient oaks which can be seen in and around the car-park to be upward of 500 years old. In replanting the park, he was anxious that his own 'little plantations shall not develop into clumps, but into groups of trees. That is to say that each tree shall keep its natural form. This entails, of course, constant thinning, a few trees every year.' As he suspected, it has not been easy to achieve this effect, but it is discernible in some of the clumps.

Below The Drive

❷ THE DRIVE

The shady evergreen drive passes through a clay seam, which is slightly acid despite the underlying chalk. A number of rhododendrons are planted here, timed for successive flowering rather than a sea of colour. The subdued evergreen feel of this area is completed by plantings of Highclere hollies (*Ilex* × *altaclarensis* 'Camelliifolia'), *Cephalotaxus*, *Podocarpus* and Italian cypresses. Only when the bend is reached does the mood lighten, as the house is revealed to the right and the North Vista to the left.

Numbers refer to bird's-eye view of the garden on the inside front cover.

❸ THE NORTH VISTA

Framed by yew trees, a fine urn forms a focal point with discrete views into the North Park and beyond.

❹ THE AUTUMN BORDER

Created originally to replace a weed-infested herbaceous border, this area contains hardy *Fuchsias; Agapanthus*, *Buddlejas*, *Hydrangea aspera* (Villosa group) and a number of varieties of *Hibiscus* and *Abelia* for later display. It also sustains interest through the earlier part of the season with a show of daffodils, *Potentillas*, the beauty bush (*Kolkwitzia*) and scented *Philadelphus*. Later colours tend to be in the white, pink, purple and blue range. Half-way along this border is a gate which provides a glimpse into the Walled Garden.

Below The Walled Garden

❺ THE WALLED GARDEN

The Walled Garden reopened to the public in 2006 after having been leased for a number of years. Traditionally, there was a fully functioning kitchen garden that produced fruit, vegetables and cut flowers for the house. The espalier fruit trees that line the central path are remnants of this time. Following a period of restoration, part of the garden is now used to grow food and flowers, and produce is often available at the shop.

❻ THE EXTERIOR

Hinton Ampner, as rebuilt by Trenwith Wells for Ralph Dutton in 1960, is a small neo-Georgian manor house in the Hampshire vernacular style. The quiet, dignified exterior gives no clue to the range and splendour of its contents.

Ralph Dutton was a man of sure eye and fine aesthetic judgement, which are reflected in the decoration and furnishing of his home.

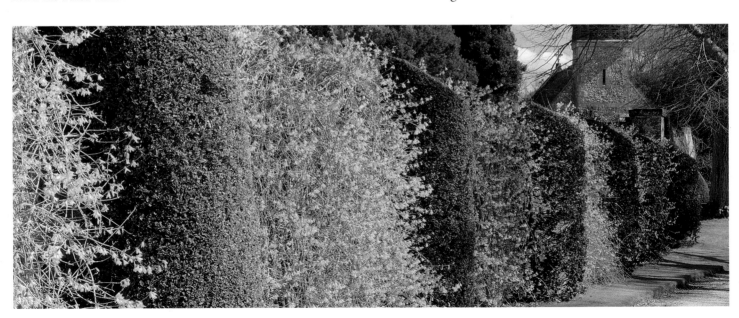

TOUR OF THE HOUSE

THE ENTRANCE HALL

This light and airy interior, with its four scagliola (imitation marble) columns and black and white marble floor, immediately sets the tone for the rest of the house, which Ralph Dutton intended to be 'aesthetic' rather than 'sporting'.

The porphyry *chimneypiece* came from one of the greatest Scottish country houses, Hamilton Palace in Lanarkshire, and required major restoration after the fire. Many similar fittings were acquired from equally important houses, as was much of the furniture.

Pictures

Ralph Dutton was particularly fond of 17th- and 18th-century Italian subject paintings, which could be bought quite cheaply from London dealers from the 1930s to the 1960s. Fine examples here include Giovanni Antonio Pellegrini's voyeuristic *Selene and Endymion* (a beautiful shepherd boy is visited every night by Selene, goddess of the moon) and *Susannah and the Elders*.

Furniture and ornaments

By the fireplace stands a pair of flat *painted figures* of a boy and girl. Known as dummy boards or silent companions, they were made in Holland in the mid-17th century. It has been suggested that they were meant to deter burglars, but they were probably just intended as decoration. Dutton used the Regency mahogany *wine-cooler* to display shrubs. He gilded the 18th-century Italian *torchères* (lamp stands) flanking the central door to the Library and displayed bowls of gilded fruit on them.

Under the stairs is an early 17th-century *marble tabletop* inlaid with semi-precious stones. The top was made in the Florentine workshops founded by Grand Duke Ferdinando I de' Medici in 1589. The supporting table is French, *c.*1710.

Christmas at Hinton Ampner

'We entered an imposing hall at one end of which stood a vast Xmas tree, glittering with baubles arranged for the children of his tenants … [Dutton gave] the children tea in the kitchen while their parents were entertained in the dining room.'

Sir Brinsley Ford, friend and visitor

Susannah and the Elders is an early work by the Venetian artist Giovanni Antonio Pellegrini, who visited England in 1708-13. The virtuous young Susannah is shown being ogled by the elders of the Synagogue. The subject (taken from the *Apocrypha*) was often simply an excuse to paint the female nude

THE DRAWING ROOM

After the fire, Ralph Dutton redesigned the room to match the 18th-century style of the other interiors, putting up the Regency stripe wallpaper and furnishing it with largely Georgian giltwood pieces. The decoration was chosen to match the colouring of the *c.*1820 French Savonnerie carpets. The late 18th-century doorcases and marble chimneypieces came from Ashburnham Place in Sussex.

The great perfectionist

'Ralph was the greatest perfectionist that I have ever known, and although he delegated the task to a professional decorator, he saw to it that every detail in the adornment of his house, from the tassel on a blind, to the fringe on a chair should be as perfect as possible.'

Sir Brinsley Ford

Pictures

The paintings include mainly Italian landscapes and English portraits. Dutton also collected scenes of Victorian life, such as *The Marriage of the Princess Royal*, who was the eldest daughter of Queen Victoria. This preliminary sketch was painted, probably during the wedding ceremony itself in 1858, by John Phillip, RA, who was better known for his romantic depictions of Spanish life. The finished painting is in the Royal Collection at Buckingham Palace.

Furniture

The 18th-century ebonised *cabinets* flanking the bay window are decorated with inlay in the style of the great 17th-century French cabinetmaker André-Charles Boulle. The *table* in the centre of the room supports an inlaid marble top made in Florence in the 17th century.

Below The *silver plaques* of reclining figures on the ebonised cabinet were made about 1580 in Augsburg in southern Germany, which attracted the best goldsmiths in Europe at that time. The twisted rock crystal columns were carved around the same date, but the whole piece was not put together until about 1875

An 18th-century air-freshener

This cassoulet or perfume-burner was made about 1770–1, at the height of 'vasemania', by the great Birmingham manufacturer Matthew Boulton. It comprises a vase of bluejohn (Derbyshire fluorspar) supported by three ormolu (gilt-bronze) griffins, which were designed by George III's favourite architect, William Chambers. This elegant Neo-classical ornament also had a practical purpose – as the 18th-century equivalent of the air-freshener. Boulton's patron Elizabeth Montagu confirmed 'how agreeable the aromatic gales are from these Cassolettes when they drive away the vapour of soup and all the fulsome savour of Dinner'.

Ralph Dutton writer

Dutton wrote a series of lively books on subjects he loved, starting with *The English Country House* in 1935 and including *The English Garden* (1937) and *The English Interior* (1948).

'In the library every book was destroyed ... subjected to intense heat and water, [they] had become almost petrified as if engulfed by a volcanic eruption, and had to be hewn out of the bookcases with pickaxes.'

Ralph Dutton

THE LIBRARY

The fire was started here by a spark from the fireplace, and entirely destroyed the porphyry chimneypiece. It was replaced with another, possibly from Marie-Antoinette's palace at St Cloud, to which Napoleon's initial 'N' and crown had been added. The pilasters between the bookcases were painted to resemble porphyry. The reliefs over the doors feature Neo-classical griffins.

Books

After the fire, Ralph Dutton set about re-creating his book collection to fill the shelves of the new Library. He bought fine editions of the great English poets, novelists and travel writers. There are also key reference works to support his career as a writer, and handsomely illustrated folios that reflect his interest in 18th-century architecture, interior design, travel and garden history. These include Buffon's sixteen-volume *Natural History* (1797–1808) with hand-coloured engravings, and a run of Sowerby's *English Botany*. Not surprisingly, he also acquired Ackermann's *Repository of Arts*, the aquatint illustrations in which provide such a vivid picture of Ralph Dutton's favourite Regency era.

Pictures

Over the fireplace, Francesco Fontebasso's *Esther fainting before Ahasuerus* shows Queen Esther interceding with her husband, the Persian King, to prevent the massacre of the Jews. Fontebasso was an 18th-century Venetian painter of the kind specially favoured by Ralph Dutton.

Ornaments

Complementing the painted porphyry pilasters between the bookcases are numerous ornaments made from real porphyry: notably, the pairs of vases on the mantelpiece and the Egyptian porphyry and ormolu urns on the tables between the windows.

Right An Egyptian Revival urn

THE SITTING ROOM

The firemen and staff from the house and garden managed to rescue most of the contents of this room by passing them out through the windows before it was destroyed. The marble fireplace, from the Adam brothers' demolished Adelphi Terrace in London, also survived intact.

Ornaments

On the mantelpiece are displayed three Louis XVI-style *urns*, made from 'bluejohn' (a fluorspar mined at Castleton in Derbyshire and popular for 18th-century ornaments) and mounted with ormolu. Either side of the fireplace hangs a set of four oval *plaques* in Wedgwood's black basaltes ware.

Pictures

The paintings are mostly 18th-century Venetian pastoral landscapes and subject pictures, but on either side of the exit door are *roundels* painted about 1785–6 by the Swiss artist Henry Fuseli, who had settled in Britain five years earlier. They depict scenes from Shakespeare's *The Winter's Tale* and are early examples of the late 18th-century vogue for illustrating Shakespeare.

Above Scene from *The Winter's Tale*, painted by Henry Fuseli

Above Ram's-head decoration on an armchair

15

Passion for porphyry

Dutton had a passion for porphyry. This purple volcanic rock had been especially prized by the Romans for its rarity, hardness and polished beauty. In their time it was to be found in only one remote site, in the Eastern Desert of Egypt. The Byzantine emperors of Constantinople loved porphyry so much that they claimed an imperial monopoly of it. From the Middle Ages onwards, surviving pieces of Roman porphyry came to symbolise the lost grandeur of Classical Antiquity. No 18th-century connoisseur's collection was complete without a porphyry urn or bust. Dutton was fascinated by porphyry's classical associations, collecting table ornaments, busts and whole chimneypieces made from the stone.

Left The Sitting Room

THE DINING ROOM

The plasterwork ceiling was rescued in 1940 from 38 Berkeley Square, the town house designed by Robert Adam for the Child family of Osterley Park, Middlesex (now also in the care of the National Trust). The artist Elizabeth Biddulph repainted the roundels after the originals were destroyed by the fire, which also consumed half of the ceiling.

Furniture

The giltwood *pier-glass* opposite the fireplace was designed in 1773 by Robert Adam for another now-demolished London mansion, Derby House in Grosvenor Square. The pair to it is also in a National Trust house, Basildon Park in Berkshire.

In the niche facing the windows is an ebony inlaid mahogany *sideboard* in the Egyptian style that became fashionable across Europe following Napoleon's invasion of Egypt in 1798 and which was particularly promoted in Britain by the designer Thomas Hope. Such bulky furniture went out of fashion in the early 20th century: Ralph Dutton picked up this piece for only £8 during the Second World War.

Under the sideboard is a large mahogany *wine-cooler* on wheels, also in Hope's Egyptian style.

Pictures

Over the mantelpiece is a copy of Zoffany's *Dutton Family*, which depicts 18th-century ancestors of Ralph Dutton playing cards.

Below right An Empire-style ormolu and glass *tazza* (dish on stand)

Below The giltwood pier-glass was designed by Robert Adam in 1773 for Derby House in Grosvenor Square, London

A Christmas lunch at Hinton Ampner

'We started with some kind of fish soufflé, then pheasant with a wonderful variety of vegetables, then Xmas pudding and mince pies with brandy butter which, when properly made, is a rare delicacy. Some first-rate cheeses to choose from, and with it all some excellent burgundy. An elderly butler was in attendance.'

Sir Brinsley Ford

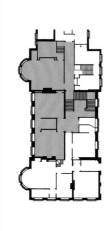

THE STAIRS

The Victorian staircase was completely destroyed by the fire. Dutton rebuilt it in the same position, but in a simpler and more graceful style. It also stopped at the first floor, as Dutton did away with the former attic storey.

THE FIRST FLOOR

Dutton took the precaution of rebuilding the house with fireproof concrete floors, supported on steel joists. A central passage connects all the bedrooms, each of which had its own *en suite* bathroom. At the far end he inserted a niche, which was painted to resemble *verde antico* (mottled green) marble as a contrast with the white marble urn he placed in it. The cabinet in the corridor displays some of the best of Dutton's important collection of ceramics.

'The men were always given breakfast in their bedrooms. It would appear on a tray with a little Louis XV coffee-pot and porcelain and linen that would have been acceptable to Madame de Pompadour.'

Sir Brinsley Ford

Left Ralph Dutton's Bedroom

RALPH DUTTON'S BEDROOM

Ralph Dutton's bedroom occupies the west side of the south front, with fine views from the generous bay window over the garden and the valley beyond. Dutton lowered the bedroom floors slightly so that the windows would fit more elegantly.

THE SOUTH BEDROOM

This was the principal guest bedroom. The marble chimneypiece featuring a eagle with a snake in its beak is one of the most elaborate and unusual in the house.

THE BATHROOM

Dutton provided the new bathrooms with all mod cons. His own is cunningly top-lit. The fashion for black bathrooms had been pioneered in the 1930s by the Surrealist patron and collector Edward James of West Dean, who commissioned one for his wife, the dancer Tilly Losch.

Above Dried-flower picture in the South Bedroom
Below Ralph Dutton's Bathroom

TOUR OF THE GARDEN

❼ THE LILY POND

Ralph Dutton laid out this area on his father's croquet lawn: 'I am inclined to doubt whether he would consider it an improvement.' The bed of white 'Iceberg' roses gives it a certain symmetry, balancing the long rectangular pond in the centre. Nine different varieties of Water Lily are planted here, and a considerable number of goldfish and Golden Orfe thrive despite the green water, which seems to protect them from herons. The 'Iceberg' roses are underplanted with mauve *Verbena rigida*, which in good years flowers with the first flush of the roses, and lasts until the repeat flowering in September.

❽ THE PAVED TERRACE

Together with the Main Terrace below, the plantings here were intended to provide 'a leafy and mellow-coloured podium from which the house rises'. Immediately under the house it is possible to grow a few slightly more tender plants than would survive elsewhere in this surprisingly cold, wet and windy garden. Plants include a selection of *Abelias* for late flower and scent, *Buddleja lindleyana* and *B. loricara* and various *Phlomis, Hoheria, Olearias* and *Salvias* beneath climbers and wall shrubs such as *Magnolia grandiflora, Azara microphylla, Campsis radicans, Fremontodendron* 'California Glory', *Solanum, Wisteria* and *Clematis armandii*.

Left Water Lily 'Attraction' in the Lily Pond
Right The Lily Pond

In Ralph Dutton's day the paving was much more heavily planted, and photographs show him standing with guests ankle-deep in plants growing in gaps between the York stone slabs. The crevices have now been replanted with an interesting variety of carpeting plants and undemanding alpines, to leave a meandering plant-free walkway along its length.

❾ THE MAIN TERRACE

Plants must be chosen carefully for this border, as it is not nearly as warm as the one under the house, because the soil consists in the main of heavy clay in the full face of the prevailing wind. The structure is provided by some relatively hardy smaller shrubs such as *Philadelphus, Viburnum* and *Fuchsia*, with some strategically placed slightly more tender types like *Buddleja crispa, Lespedeza bicolor* and various *Cistus*. Planting spaces are also left for tender summer perennials, including *Argyranthemums* in profusion and a number of *Penstemons* and *Verbenas*. September flowering is particularly good here with some fine *Hibiscus* and *Gladiolus callianthus* 'Murieliae' amongst many other plants of interest.

Elegance and shape

'We were all most impressed by the way the garden is kept up. The lawns are like carpets and mown in straight lines to give them a pattern, while the yew hedges are clipped with a skill which gives them an elegance and shape echoing the malachite vases within the house.'

Sir Brinsley Ford

🔟 THE SUNKEN GARDEN

This was the first area planned by Ralph Dutton in 1935 and is punctuated by the topiary which is such an identifying feature of Hinton Ampner. Once again, the soil here is very heavy, wet and cold in the winter, and the southerly aspect turns it from uncomfortably hot in the summer to exposed and windswept through the closed season. So it is difficult to support many of the plants which were once grown here. The raised beds now display *Alliums* for late-spring interest and an excellent selection of perennials for mid- and late-summer effect, with a range of *Penstemons* and *Salvias*, including the black-flowered *S. discolor*, the mauve and white *S. leucantha*, the delicate *S. elegans* and some imposing blue varieties at the back of the border.

The formal beds in the centre are traditionally filled with *Dahlia* 'Fascination' in the summer and a variety of tulips and forget-me-nots in the spring.

1️⃣1️⃣ THE LONG WALK

This perfectly straight path 180 metres long links the extremities of the garden from west to east. The shade cast by an avenue of 30 clipped Irish Yews changes the character of the west end of the walk through the day as the sun passes across the sky. The formal plantings of the Sunken Garden give a glimpse of colour at the half-way point on the walk, enticing you along, and as you stroll from one end to the other you will have passed no fewer than seven exit points

Top A raised bed in the Sunken Garden

Left The Sunken Garden in spring

leading in different directions, all of which are invisible from either end. Behind the Irish Yews lies the shrub rose border, completed in 1954 and containing many types of rose employed particularly with fragrance in mind. These include hybrid musks such as 'Cornelia', 'Penelope' and 'Felicia', the gallicas *Rosa mundi* and 'Tuscany', albas ('Céleste', 'Queen of Denmark') and bourbons ('Mme Isaac Pereire').

Focal points are a marble statue of Diana against an Irish Yew and the sundial centred on an earlier beech tree in the park.

🄬 THE PARK

Access to the Park can be gained via the cattle-grids at the west end of the Long Walk and at the top of the Lime Avenue.

Above The statue of Diana on the Long Walk

Decently hid

Let not each beauty ev'ry
    where be spy'd
Where half the skill is
    decently to hide;
He gains all points, who
    pleasingly confounds,
Surprizes, varies, and
    conceals the Bounds.

Alexander Pope

Left Dahlia 'Fascination'

Above There are fine views from the Bastion over the surrounding countryside

⑬ THE SOUTH PATH

The modesty of Ralph Dutton's design demands that the colourful South Border, with its roses, *Buddleja alternifolia* and *Philadelphus* underplanted with hardy geraniums and artemisias, should be screened from view by a hedge on the south side. He was as concerned to set his house and garden unobtrusively within the rural landscape as he was to make use of the setting from within the garden. Other plants of interest in this border include the large cream-flowered lilac, *Syringa reticulata* var. *mandschurica*.

⑭ THE BASTION

This was one of the last features to be finished and allows an uninterrupted view across the countryside to the south. The semicircular design encourages you to look in all directions. From here you can also see how the Lime Avenue has been clumped to form three informal groups of trees. This presumably took place when the avenue ceased to serve as the main entrance with the demolition of the Tudor house in 1793.

Left The Temple

⓯ THE TEMPLE

Built as a folly, gazebo and resting-place, the Temple is rather awkwardly placed, as it tries to align itself not only with the east–west Long Walk, but also with the north–south axis of the entrance drive to the Tudor building. The focal point of the obelisk rewards the curious by giving views back to the house, which illustrate Dutton's concern to ensure that his garden appeared as an organic component of its surroundings.

The borders here serve both as a windbreak and to provide pockets of colour throughout the season, as the many different shrubs flower and fade in turn.

⓰ THE AVENUE

The lime trees retain the character of an avenue when seen from either end, despite having been clumped. This feature was incorporated into the garden during the Second World War at the request of the headmistress of Portsmouth High School, which had been evacuated here. It seems that the younger gardeners were proving too much of a distraction for her schoolgirls, and Dutton was encouraged to find a project for them away from the house. This request coincided happily with plans he already had for the area.

Above The Avenue

17 THE TENNIS COURT PATH

The soil here is relatively light compared with much of the garden, and although its original purpose was to provide a windbreak, there are some good lilacs here, a substantial stand of *Phlomis russeliana*, various *Cistus* and *Hebes*, as well as *Buddleja* × *pikei* 'Hever'.

18 THE YEW GARDEN

Created in its present form as a replacement for Ralph Dutton's mother's persistently failing rose garden, this feature exhibits tulips and forget-me-nots in the spring in various colour schemes, usually chosen to be light and airy within the dark formality of the yew hedging. The summer schemes have made use of *Dahlias*, *Heliotropes* and *Salvias*, normally favouring subtle and subdued tones. The cutaway hedge frames the horse chestnut at the far end of the terrace, and in turn the tree is pruned into an arch over the statue, which is silhouetted against the sky. Turning to look down the steps in the opposite direction, the eye is led between the Irish Yews, over the gate, to a clump of *Acer platanoides* 'Schwedleri' in the distance, which provides a natural but constantly changing point of reference.

⓳ THE PHILADELPHUS WALK

The huge Russian Vine marks the start of this path, which for a couple of all-too-short weeks in summer is filled with cascades of white *Philadelphus* nodding over the tall box hedging. The muted tones and pleasant scents impart a great tranquillity to this walk.

⓴ THE DELL

Deliberately not signalled by any feature, the Dell was conceived as an intimate and separate space, differing in atmosphere from all the other areas of the garden.

The first attempts at a chalk garden of tender plants failed because this is a frost pocket. The subsequent scheme for a foliage garden also deteriorated over the years, as one of the feature plants was the dangerous Giant Hogweed, which was allowed to self-seed, rendering the borders unmaintainable. The restored garden of today consists of foliage plants, which are more manageable, and are

Below The Philadelphus Walk

planted and maintained higher up the banks than before. To retain the sense of tranquillity, the plants have been chosen to demonstrate great variety of shape, texture and form, but it remains a predominantly green oasis with few contrasts of foliage colour. Again, in keeping with Dutton's original planting and because of the isolated nature of this space, some of the colour scheme departs from his overall preference for pastel shades. So here bright orange, red and gold punctuation marks can be seen at times from such plants as *Lilium henryi*, *Ligularia* 'Desdemona', *Hemerocallis*, *Crocosmia* 'Lucifer' and *Inula magnifica*. There is also a collection of Foxglove trees (*Paulownia*),

Rodgersias and some attractive grasses. Bold foliage effects are created by *Rheums*, *Darmera peltata* and *Hostas*. The 'Kiftsgate' and *brunonii* roses are spectacular in flower and hip.

㉑ THE DELL VIEW PATH

A narrow shady path provides the surprise of glimpses into the Dell from above, as well as containing some interesting plants, including *Idesia polycarpa*, the scented *Viburnum* 'Aurora', *V. × carlcephalum* and a Tulip Tree (*Liriodendron tulipifera*).

Below The entrance to the Dell

22 THE EAST LAWN

'At Hinton I am inclined to believe that the most attractive area is the sward of plain lawn lying between the church and the house with the tall jade-green stems of beech trees rising beyond it. There is spaciousness and tranquillity here, which my more elaborate efforts elsewhere have not achieved.'

Ralph Dutton

This quotation is perhaps over-modest, but there is an attractive simplicity to this area which comes to life in spring when carpets of bulbs fill the long grass areas.

The bed near the church is partly planted to provide winter and early season scent for the congregation of the church, and contains *Sarcococcas*, *Daphnes* and Hyacinths.

Opposite The Orchard in spring
Below Orchard blossom

Below The Orchard with the bell-tower of All Saints church

23 THE CHURCH

All Saints parish church is originally Saxon. The chancel was rebuilt before 1822, and the nave by Ralph Dutton's grandfather in the 1870s, when the French-style bell-tower was also added. Ralph Dutton and many of his ancestors are buried here.

24 THE ORCHARD

The contrast between the precisely clipped formality of the hedging and the spring bulb area within is most marked in July, after the bulb foliage has died back, and just before the grass is cut. It typifies Dutton's preference for a formal structure softened with an informality of plantings behind. Early colour comes from species crocuses, followed by Narcissi with *Anemone blanda* and *A. nemorosa*. The white and pink cherries are followed by apple and quince blossom, and cow parsley completes the spring season. Carpets of autumn-flowering *Crocus speciosus* bring the area back to life in late September.

25 THE MAGNOLIA GARDEN

On the relatively deep, slightly acid soil of this area, plants are grown which would not tolerate the alkalinity of the rest of the garden. Here Ralph Dutton was able to construct a shady ericaceous woodland walk where *Camellias*, *Azaleas*, *Eucryphias*, *Enkianthus*, *Pieris*, *Magnolias*, *Zenobia*, *Chionanthus* and a number of *Hydrangeas* for later flowering can all be seen growing, creating a mood very different from the rest of Hinton Ampner.

THE ESTATE

The estate had been in the possession of the Stawell and Dutton families for 400 years when Ralph Dutton bequeathed it to the National Trust in 1985. The estate consists of 1,650 acres (663 hectares) of chalk farm and woodland, and includes the hamlet of Hinton Ampner.

The entire estate is a rare example of 'improvement' in the 18th-century manner carried out in the 20th century. The park and estate were planted to enhance the picturesque nature of the views from the house and the landscape generally. Ralph Dutton had begun his replanting of the estate and remodelling of the house in the 1930s. The entire project was managed with a combination of fine aesthetic sensibility and a sure eye. Ralph Dutton had published widely on English houses and gardens, and his revival of the Hinton estate was inspired by his deep knowledge and love of all aspects of the 18th century.

Below The park